Tao of Chinese Mandalas

An Adult Colouring Book of Zen Mindfulness

© Charles Chan 2017

TA☯WAY

Taoway Publishing - www.taoway.co.uk

1st Edition March 2017

ISBN 978-0-9957419-1-1

This colouring book belongs to

MANDALAS 1 - 8

 Spring

 Summer

 Autumn

 Winter

 6 Buddha Mudras 1

 6 Buddha Mudras 2

 Vitarka Mudra

 Namaskara Mudra

MANDALAS 9 - 28

Blessing, Longevity, Clouds, Interlocking Rings

Floral Vine, Happiness, Blessing and Lucky Bats, Floral Peaches

Floral Butterfly, Happiness, Tai Chi, Floral Vine

Floral Vine, Longevity, Clouds, Floral Hearts

Happiness and Lucky Bats Square

Floral Tiled Square

Longevity and Floral Tiled Square

Longevity and Floral Vine Square

Floral Vine Formation Square 1

Floral Vine Formation Square 2

Floral Vine Formation Square 3

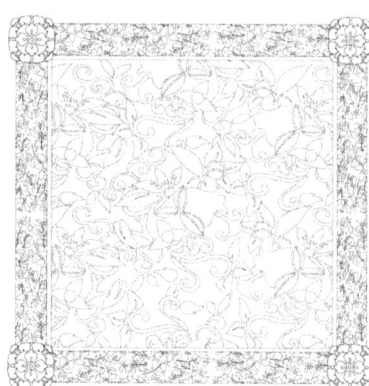

Floral Vine Formation Square 4

Dragon and Fire Pearl

Phoenix

Mosaic Dragon and Fire Pearl

Tiger

MANDALAS 37 - 44

Floral Mosaic and
Spring Birds

Blessing and Lucky
Bats

Floral Formation and
Longevity

Floral Formation and
Peaches

Blessing

Buddhist Lotus

Lucky Bats and
Celestial Clouds

Rattan Thatch

INTRODUCTION

Welcome to the new Era of Adult Colouring Phenomenon

I can fondly remember that colouring was one of my favourite hobbies when I was a child. Colouring books in those days were exclusively designed for children and colouring media were limited to mainly pencils, watercolours and wax crayons. Times have changed, as a new trend of colouring books for adults has become a very popular trend. With that, the colouring media have also expanded with an array of new felt pens, gel pens, colour ball pens and water-soluble colour crayons that are flooding the market to meet this new craze. Colouring for adults is not merely a hobby, it has turned into new 20th century self-help, de-stress therapy. Some people even use it as a vehicle of attaining mindfulness and it has become a new modality of mindful meditation.

Hephzibah Kaplan, director at the London Art Therapy Centre believes colouring is very similar to reciting a meditation mantra inducing a meditative, mindful state. A conventional meditation approach of both Eastern and Western denominations focuses attention actively on simple repetitive tasks such as reciting a mantra, chanting, striking a bell at certain momentum or breathing rhythmically in a certain sequence. These are all aim to heighten your concentration and awareness on the moment and help you let go of your everyday stress and negative thoughts. When you are deeply focused, you lose yourself into a mindful reverie; a sense of tranquillity will emerge. However, some people may find it hard to actively focus on something abstract; colouring is an easier alternative to induce a mindful state of consciousness because it can gently and effortlessly create the focus and block out the intrusive thoughts. As you are colouring small shapes of confined areas, your mind will involuntarily focus onto the areas you are working at.

Colouring is a life enriching hobby

Whether you are a professional artist or an absolute beginner, you can take on this enjoyable and relaxing hobby and get the most profound benefits for your body, mind and spirit. If you are an experienced artist, colouring gives you an alternative structure to experiment with your skills. If you are a novice, you can learn the craft by trial and error and experimentation. Like all creative activities, colouring brings out your hidden artistic inspirations, your appreciation to beauty, your sensitivity to colours, contrast and shapes and your creative ingenuity of mixing and combining the colours for your composition. It provides a platform for your journey of self-reflection, self-discovery and self-actualisation. It is a very enjoyable and relaxing experience, especially when you can get into the zone of deep mindful concentration. It provides you with personal space and time for you to explore your real self in a deeper and meaningful way. It gives you a sense of purpose and a direction when engaging with a colouring project, something to target for and to accomplish. Finally, it gives you a sense of achievement and deep satisfaction when the task is accomplished, and the masterpiece can be admired by yourself, your family and friends or other fellow colourists.

Coloring can lower blood pressure

Coloring does not have a direct curative effect on lowering your blood pressure, but it does have a profound effect of lowering anxiety, reducing your stress level and calming your mind. When your mind is peaceful and tranquil, your heart beats slower and your breathing becomes longer and deeper which will signal the body to turn off the 'fight or flight' mode. If you are interested in a natural therapy of curing high blood pressure, you can take reference from my other publication, "Lowering High Blood Pressure with Acupressure: Normalising your blood pressure in 30 minutes naturally without prescription drugs" which is available in both kindle and physical book formats at:

https://www.amazon.co.uk/Lowering-High-Blood-Pressure-Acupressure/dp/0995741905 in the UK
or
https://www.amazon.com/Lowering-High-Blood-Pressure-Acupressure/dp/0995741905 in the US

Alzheimer and Dementia

According to the Alzheimer's Association, "Art projects and colouring can create a sense of accomplishment and purpose and they provide Alzheimer and Dementia sufferers with an opportunity for making meaningful self-expression, and establishing their self-worthiness and dignity." Studies show that by encouraging people to doodle and shade in the printed shapes while a list of random names was read aloud, those people remembered 29% more names than those who didn't doodle. Therefore, colouring may also help Alzheimer and Dementia sufferers improve their memory and cognitive functions.

Colouring improves sleep

As we have already discussed, colouring can help to alleviate stress and anxiety. People who suffer from insomnia may be due to anxiety and stress of their everyday lives. If they colour before bedtime, it will greatly help them reduce their anxiety and stress level. Colouring puts your mind into a tranquil meditative state; a state which is more allied to the sleeping state of consciousness.

ABOUT MANDALAS

My mandalas were cryptograms concerning the state of self which were presented to me anew each day. In them I saw the self - that is, my whole being - actively at work. To be sure, at first I could only dimly understand them; but they seemed to me highly significant, and I guarded them like precious pearls. I had the distinct feeling that they were something central, and in time I acquired through them a living conception of the self. The self, I thought, was like the monad which I am, and which is my world. The mandala represents this monad, and corresponds to the microcosmic nature of the psyche.

Carl Jung

Carl Jung believed mandalas were archetypal symbols; the psychological expression of the totality of the self which belongs to the collective unconscious of the cosmic totality. Often mandalas are represented by circles and squares. If a circle appears inside a square, it signifies as the universal symbol of wholeness. Coincidentally, in the Chinese language, it also refers to the sky as round and earth as square. Jung believed that the central point of a mandala is a symbol of the centre of our being, a still and calm point about which the chaotic elements and emotional turmoil of our lives revolve. Creating or colouring mandalas is a gateway to get in touch with our centre of peace and stillness and bring order to resolve our internal turmoil and chaos.

SYMBOLS USED IN CHINESE MANDALAS

Chinese mandalas are composed of an array of cultural, mythological and religious symbols. Very often, these symbols signify good fortune, happiness, longevity and wealth. The designs and the symbolism always echo the Taoist principles of balance and harmony. Here are some of the frequently used symbols in the Chinese mandala designs:

Dragon and Phoenix

Dragon and Phoenix often appear together in the Chinese mandalas. They are the archetypal symbols of the Yin and Yang polarities of the universal oneness, the totality, procreation and harmony of the universe. The Dragon symbolises masculine energy and virility. The Phoenix symbolises the feminine splendour and beauty. They often represent a perfect union of a marriage that is blessed with success and prosperity as well as giving birth to many offspring.

- 龍 Dragons are considered celestial emperors who can command wind, thunders, waves, sunshine and rain. They are the gods and guardians of the forces of Mother Nature. The Chinese Dragons are looked upon as the ultimate symbol of extremely good fortune. The mystical power of the Dragons can ward off evil spirits and attract fortune. Whoever wears Dragon artifices or clothing with Dragon symbols will be blessed with safety, good health and great prosperity. Traditionally, Chinese emperors are believed to be an incarnation of Dragons. They wore Dragon robes and filled their palaces with Dragon paintings, sculptures and symbols. Chinese people pride themselves as 龍的傳人 the "Descendants of the Dragon" as a symbol of ethnic identity.

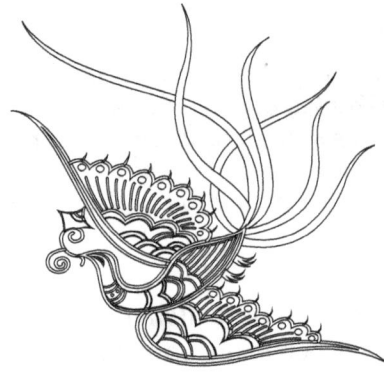

- 凤凰 Phoenix, on the other hand, represents the goddess of all the winged creatures. Phoenix sometimes represents the Yin energy. This heavenly bird will harvest opportunity luck, success and prosperity. The Phoenix is capable of turning misfortune into opportunity and good luck. It could mysteriously carve out a path of opportunities for your business, work, career or any other pursuits in your life. Phoenix is associated with the south corner in the Feng Shui philosophy (the science of placement) which brings you fame and popularity. It represents best side of the feminine quality, such as meekness, kindness, submissiveness, sensuality, fertility and maternal love.

蝙蝠 Bats are considered to be blessings and prosperity because the second Chinese syllable of bat is pronounced as Fu which is similar to the pronunciation of blessing and prosperity.

A mandala of five bats (五福臨門 The Entrance of five blessings) is often presented as the most auspicious symbol at all times. The five blessings are:

- 長壽 Longevity
- 富貴 Wealth
- 康寧 Peace
- 好德 Good Virtue
- 善終 Natural Death

福 *Fu Character*

Fu can be translated as blessing or good fortune. There are many different variants of the writing. It is one of the most popular Chinese characters during the Chinese New Year period. It is often posted upside down on the front door, to signify good fortune has arrived. This is because the character 到 "arrive" and the character 倒 "upside down" share the similar phonetic sound.

喜 *Xi Character*

Xi can be translated as happiness or joyfulness. There are many variations of artistic design of the Xi character. Very often they appear as double happiness, especially when there is a wedding occasion.

寿 *Shou Character*

Shou can be translated as longevity. Again, there are many variants of the character. The character often appears alone in the centre of the mandala, and sometimes it is surrounded by flowers, bats, or other good luck symbols, such as dragons or golden nuggets.

松竹梅 *Pine, Bamboo and Plum Blossom*

Pine is a Chinese symbol of longevity and endurance which can withstand harsh winter conditions. Similar to Pine, Bamboo is another symbol of longevity, endurance and flexibility. Plum is also another symbol of longevity, resilience and endurance because plum trees can grow for a long time and bloom beautifully during the harsh winter months. Pine, Bamboo and Plum are often called the three friends of the winter because of their tenacity and endurance in midst of the harsh winter conditions and they are often used as the auspicious symbols for long life.

桃 *Peach*

Peach trees and peach fruits are Chinese symbols of good fortune and long life. Legend tells that the celestial peaches in the garden of Jade emperor's heavenly palace have magical powers and promote immortality.

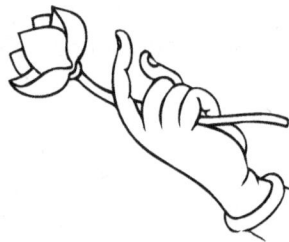

莲 *Lotus*

The lotus flower is one of the most important flowers in the Chinese religious culture. It symbolises the holy seat of Buddha because the flower rises from the mud environment and blooms in exquisite beauty without contamination by the muddy water. It symbolises purity of the heart and also represents long life and honour.

COLOURING THE FIRST TIME

If this is your first time doing adult colouring, it would be a good idea to invest in a variety of decent media. Be adventurous and experiment using new media to discover interesting effects to assure successful outcomes. Gone are the days that colouring was only confined to using colour pencils, wax crayons and water colour. New colouring media can produce very interesting, more vibrant and dynamic effects but at the same time, they can be quite challenging to handle if you are a beginner or if you are not familiar with them. There are eight Experiment Pages at the end of this book. Do make use of them freely to experiment with the media, discover their properties, work out the best colouring strategies such as the method of applying or different ways of mixing and blending. When you are familiar with the media and have developed sound techniques, you will be able to apply the media liberally and creatively onto your project with maximum confidence and certainty and minimise any unnecessary errors.

Here is the list of media you might find useful and interesting for your projects:

Water-soluble colouring pencils

This medium often comes with a large spectrum of rich and luscious colours that can be applied as you would with any traditional colouring pencils: using techniques such as dotting, hatching with one direction strokes or using backward and forward strokes; or scumbling with small circular lines. Traditional techniques are great for attaining fine details. With water-soluble colouring pencils, you can also wash over a coloured area with a tiny bit of water using a brush or a cotton bud to create a blend or wash effect. Be careful not to over-soak or over-rub the paper to avoid crinkling or damaging the paper. The colour will become permanent once it is dry and you can work over the top of the same area using different colours or a different medium.

Markers/Felt Tips/Fibre Tips

Make sure to acquiring a wide range of markers with different tip shapes, sizes and hardness. Different types of tip can give you different colouring effects and precision. When colouring with a wet medium like markers, make sure to test the extent of bleeding they could produce and the consistency of mixing/blending with another medium. It might be wise to put a piece of blotting paper behind your colouring page before applying any marker on your colouring page. Also, consider using the alcohol based markers instead of the water based markers as they are a lot kinder for preserving the integrity of the paper. Water based media may mush up or crinkle paper.

Gel Ink Pens

Gel Ink Pens are the new kids on the block and they are unique with their three-dimensional, glassy and metallic effects. Technically, gel ink is a water-based ink in the form of a gel which in theory prevents the ink from soaking into the paper. However, because the ink takes much longer to dry, it can be smeared or smudged easily before it is fully dry. An advantage of using gel inks is that you can draw on top of existing coloured locations. Gel ink pens are fantastic for outlining your drawings, especially on a stained glass design to give it a more three-dimensional look and feel.

Conte Chalk/Pastels

Both powdered Conte chalk and oil pastels are great media for producing soft blending and background gradient colours. You can apply the medium using your fingers, a brush, a cotton bud or simply some cotton wool or tissue paper. Apply the colour liberally on your picture and use an eraser to correct the error, adjust the colour depth and achieve a gradual gradient tone. Don't forget to fix the chalk with a fixing agent or hair spray.

Spring

Summer

Autumn

Winter

6 Buddha Mudras 1

6 Buddha Mudras 2

Vitarka Mudra

Namaskara Mudra

Blessing, Longevity, Clouds, Interlocking Rings

Floral Vine, Happiness, Blessing and Lucky Bats, Floral Peaches

Floral Butterfly, Happiness, Tai Chi, Floral Vine

Floral Vine, Longevity, Clouds, Floral Hearts

Happiness and Lucky Bats Square

Floral Tiled Square

Longevity and Floral Tiled Square

Longevity and Floral Vine Square

Floral Vine Formation Square 1

Floral Vine Formation Square 2

Floral Vine Formation Square 3

Floral Vine Formation Square 4

Dragon and Fire Pearl

Phoenix

Mosaic Dragon and Fire Pearl

Tiger

Floral Mosaic and Spring Birds

Blessing and Lucky Bats

Floral Formation and Peaches

Blessing

Buddhist Lotus

Lucky Bats and Celestial Clouds

Rattan Thatch

Experiment Page 1

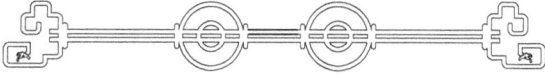

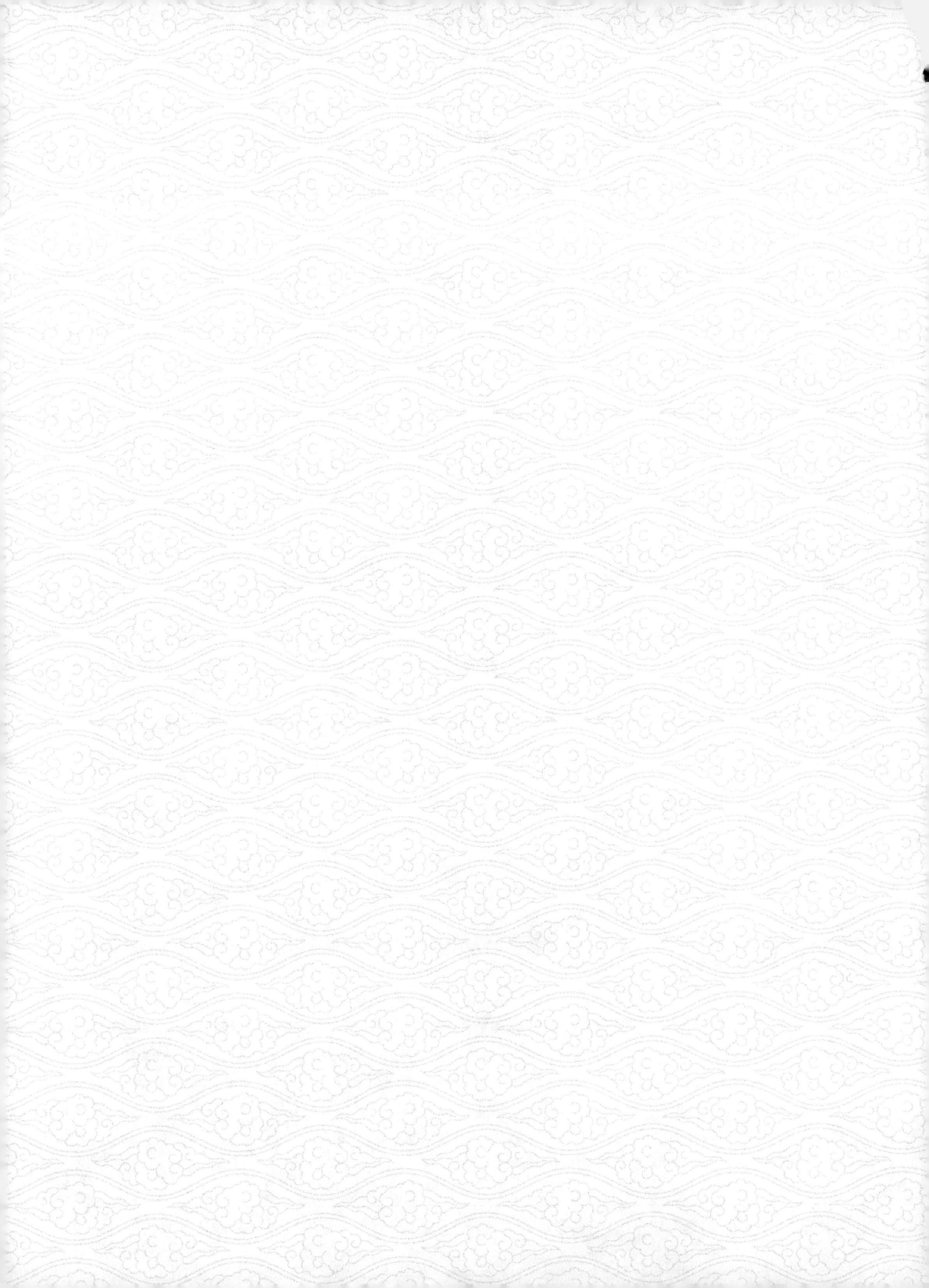

Copyright Notice

About the Author

Charles Chan is a modern Taoist, a martial artist, a sculptor, an animator, an artist of traditional Chinese ink painting, western wet and dry media painting/drawing as well as digital media. Professionally, he is a multimedia designer and a teacher at a university in the UK.

Other Publications

Lowering High Blood Pressure with Acupressure
Normalising your blood pressure in 30 minutes naturally without prescription drugs

- Kindle 2nd Edition February 2017
  Published by Amazon Kindle Direct Publishing
  ASIN: B01N0LN0IJ

- Apple iBook 1st Edition April 2017
  Published by Taoway Publishing
  ISBN 978-0-9957419-2-8

- Paperback 1st Edition February 2017
  Published by Taoway Publishing
  ISBN 978-0-9957419-0-4

The Taoist Secrets of Long Life and Good Health
A Complete Programme to Rejuvenate Mind, Body and Spirit

- Published by Godsfield Press, a division of the Octopus Publishing Group
  First Edition January 2006
  ISBN 1-84181-281-1